DISCOVERING
NEW ZEALAND
BIRDS

Sandra Morris

REED

WHAT IS A BIRD?

Birds live all over the place – by the sea, in the city and in the bush. In this book you will meet some fascinating birds, and most of them are found only in New Zealand. Some of these birds are now very rare and you will only see them if you are very lucky, but if you keep a look-out you will be able to see some of the others. Watch closely and you will see how they feed, how they fly and what sort of calls they make. When you are watching birds remember to keep still and quiet so you don't disturb them.

Although most birds have four toes, their feet can look very different. Most birds that perch in branches have three toes that point forwards and one toe that points backwards. Birds that climb trees have two toes pointing forwards and two pointing backwards. Water birds, such as ducks, have webbed toes so they can paddle.

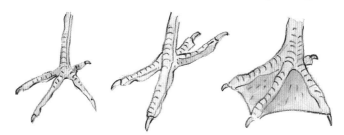

Birds use their beaks to pick up food in the same way we use our hands, and different shaped beaks or bills are useful for eating different sorts of food. The kaka uses its strong hooked beak to find grubs in rotten wood. The shag uses its long bill like tweezers to pick up small fish. The oystercatcher's thick powerful beak is good for breaking tough cockle shells and tearing out the insides.

Kaka   *Spotted Shag*   *Oystercatcher*

Birds are the only animals with feathers. Feathers keep the bird warm and dry, as well as helping it to fly. There are three kinds of feathers. Long feathers in the wings and tail are for flight. Fluffy down next to the skin keeps the bird warm, and body feathers over the top of the down keep out the rain and wind. To keep their feathers in tip-top working order birds spend a lot of their day preening and tidying their feathers.

WOOD PIGEON

Kereru, Ku Ku, Kukupa

The plump wood pigeon has feathers that shimmer and change colours in different lights.

In Maori legend the wood pigeon's colours came from the clothes Maui wore when he changed into a pigeon so he could visit the underworld to look for his parents. His white dogskin apron became the pigeon's 'singlet' of breast feathers, while his brown belt became the dark feathers around the pigeon's neck.

Wood pigeons are our largest flighted forest bird and they eat the big fruit of trees such as miro, tawa and karaka. The hard, fruity flesh around the seeds is digested in the pigeon's stomach, and eventually the seeds pass through the bird and are 'planted' throughout the forest, complete with their own pile of manure!

In spring, male wood pigeons show off to the females with stunning flying displays. They swoop up out of the forest high into the air and then plummet back towards the trees. Just missing the trees, they swoop back up again.

Wood pigeons build a very flimsy nest for their one egg. The bottom of the nest is often so thin it is surprising the egg doesn't fall through! Wood pigeons are very caring parents. While the chick is small they feed it on milk they produce in their stomach, then later on fruit pulp.

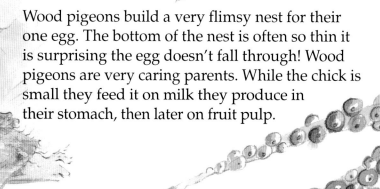

Wood pigeons used to be an important food for Maori, who would hunt them using snares and spears. They preserved the bodies in fat in gourds, and used the glossy feathers to make cloaks.

Although they hardly ever coo or call, wood pigeons can be very noisy as they crash around in the trees, especially after a huge meal of fruit. They were named ku ku after the noise their wings make as they fly.

WRYBILL

Ngutu-parore

The story of the wrybill has a strange twist to it. For the wrybill is the only bird in the world with a bent beak, that twists to the right. There are about 5000 wrybills, and all of them are in New Zealand. During autumn and winter they fly to the North Island to spend the winter feeding in big flocks on mudflats.

At low tide, when the mud is covered by a thin film of water, the wrybill's bent beak becomes a handy eating tool. The birds rush back and forth across the mud, rapidly sweeping their beaks through the water. They use their beaks as spoons to stir up the water, and then as scoops to pick up a rich soup of water and tiny shrimps. Finally, their beaks sift out the shrimps, like sieves. Sometimes they use their beaks as pincers to grab small crabs, which they also stalk across the mud.

At high tide, when the water is too deep for the wrybills to feed, they move to high shellbanks or nearby paddocks to rest.

In spring, the wrybills fly to the South Island to breed on the wide, braided rivers of the east coast. Here they use their beaks to probe and poke under and around stones. In the river, they gently feel for long mayfly larvae that hang in the water under the stones. In dry, shingle river-beds they look for small spiders and beetles hiding between the stones.

It is the male wrybill that builds the nest. He hollows out a sandy patch amongst the stones, and lines it with small pebbles. The female lays two grey-speckled eggs, which blend perfectly with the stones around them. Both parents take turns to incubate the eggs. With their grey and white feathers the wrybills are also well camouflaged, and when enemies such as gulls or harrier hawks fly past, the parents 'sit tight', and are very difficult to see.

The grey-speckled chicks are also difficult to spot amongst the stones. They are very precocious – as soon as they hatch they leave the nest and are able to feed themselves, under the watchful eye of their parents.

KINGFISHER

Kotare

The kingfisher is an excellent high diver. Always alert, this keen-eyed bird perches on a handy tree, fence post or even a telephone line, until it spots a likely meal. Then it dives down and snatches it up in its long beak.

Kingfishers really throw themselves into their nest building. They dive bomb a clay bank or a rotten tree using their large strong beak to dig out a small hole. When the hole is big enough to sit in they continue digging in a rather less frantic way, using their claws as well as their beak. At the end of a long tunnel they make a small nest chamber in which the female lays four or five eggs.

A kingfisher nest is a noisy place, with the chicks making a constant din of wheezing and rasping.

The nest is also very smelly. Kingfishers are poor housekeepers, and their nest soon becomes a mess of rotten food and droppings. It is quite easy to find such a loud, smelly nest, but luckily the chicks are safely hidden at the end of the long tunnel.

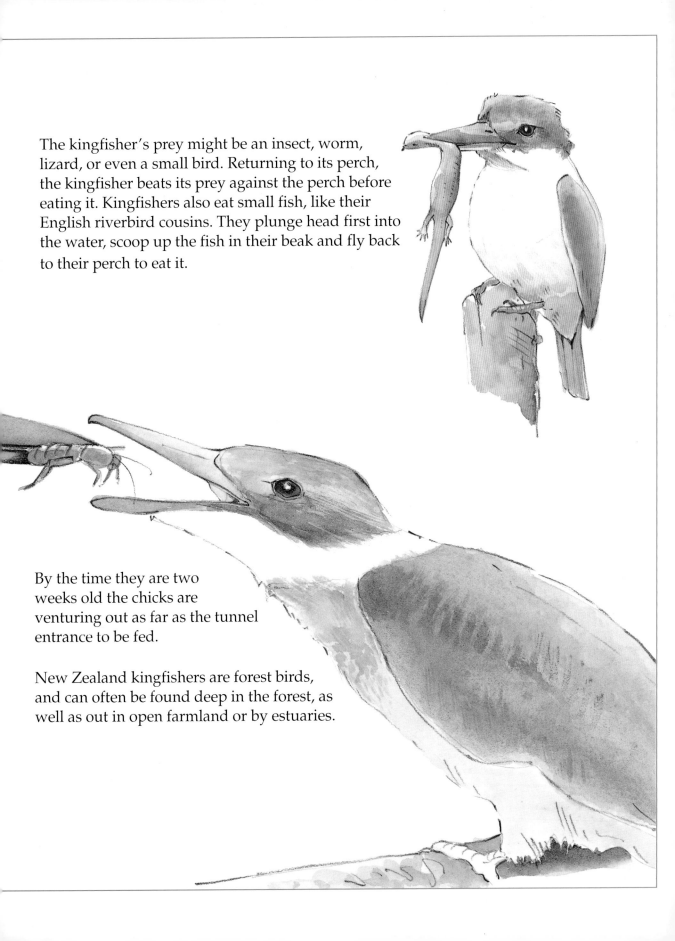

The kingfisher's prey might be an insect, worm, lizard, or even a small bird. Returning to its perch, the kingfisher beats its prey against the perch before eating it. Kingfishers also eat small fish, like their English riverbird cousins. They plunge head first into the water, scoop up the fish in their beak and fly back to their perch to eat it.

By the time they are two weeks old the chicks are venturing out as far as the tunnel entrance to be fed.

New Zealand kingfishers are forest birds, and can often be found deep in the forest, as well as out in open farmland or by estuaries.

YELLOW-EYED PENGUIN

Hoiho

The hoiho, whose name means noise shouter, is one of the world's rarest penguins. Most hoiho live on New Zealand's small southern islands, but a few hundred live on the coast of Otago and the Catlins. On some quiet beaches you can still see them surfing ashore in the evening and climbing up to their nests.

Unlike other penguins, hoiho nest on their own, out of sight of other penguins. In spring they lay two eggs in a simple nest hidden beneath a shady bush.

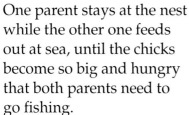

One parent stays at the nest while the other one feeds out at sea, until the chicks become so big and hungry that both parents need to go fishing.

Once the chicks have lost their baby down and left the nest, it is their parents' turn to moult. Every year all their old feathers are replaced with new ones, so their coat stays sleek and waterproof. During the three weeks it takes to moult, hoiho can't go to sea to feed, but they can live off their stored fat.

When they swim on the surface of the sea hoiho use their flippers like paddles. Underwater they move their flippers as if they were flying. When they want to get somewhere in a hurry they porpoise in and out of the water, so they can breathe while travelling fast. When they are really moving, they can reach speeds of up to 25 kilometres an hour.

Hoiho feed on small fish living on the sea floor. They are strong divers, and can make as many as 300 dives a day, returning to the surface for a few seconds between dives to breathe.

Maori legend says that once upon a time Tawaki the penguin and Toroa the albatross were arguing over who was the best at flying and fishing. Finally Tane Mahuta, God of the Forest, silenced them and gave them each a unique gift. Toroa grew the largest wings of any sea bird so it could soar over the ocean far from land, and Tawaki's wings became short, narrow flippers so it could fly beneath the ocean.

TAKAHE

In 1948, in rugged Fiordland, an Invercargill doctor made an exciting discovery – a bird that everyone thought was extinct!

Takahe live high in the mountains feeding on tussocks and mountain daisies. They pull out a long tussock stalk with their beak, hold it firmly in one claw, and snip off the juiciest bottom part before throwing the rest away. As tussock is not a very nutritious food, takahe spend a lot of time pulling and snipping tussocks. It is easy to see where takahe have been as they leave many uneaten stalks lying around, and they produce lots of droppings that look just like mini hay bales.

Tussock bushes provide shelter as well as food for the takahe, and the birds hide their nests right underneath clumps of tussock.

Unfortunately takahe numbers dropped rapidly after Dr Orbell found them. In the 1980s, when there were only about 120 birds left in the wild, scientists set about saving them. As well as killing the deer, which were eating all the takahe's food, the scientists began to raise takahe in a special captive rearing unit.

Each spring scientists visit takahe nests to collect one of the two eggs usually laid. One egg is left for the parents to look after. The collected eggs are placed in an incubator and tapes of takahe noises are played to them. After they hatch the chicks are put in a cage with a 'foster mum', who is really a heated, life size takahe model. The chicks can sit under her to stay safe and warm. They are fed baby food by another 'parent' who is really a human hand in a 'takahe' glove puppet.

The takahe chicks are never allowed to see the people who look after them in case they begin to think they are humans and not birds!

By winter, the young takahe are big enough to be put outside in a tussock reserve. Here they learn to eat tussocks and dig up fern roots, just as they will need to do in the mountains. The following year the young takahe are moved back to the mountains to join the wild birds.

BLACK ROBIN

The black robin was once the rarest bird in the world. In 1979 there were only five black robins left, and they would have become extinct if it hadn't been for a miracle.

For over a hundred years a small population of black robins had survived on the top of a steep, windy island. This was Little Mangere Island, which lies in the middle of the ocean, hundreds of kilometres east of New Zealand.

In the 1970s, however, something went very wrong. The forest was being eroded and damaged by wind, and the black robin's food and shelter were vanishing. The robin began to vanish too, so the birds were taken to a larger island called Mangere. But this move wasn't successful, and soon only five birds remained. Then a scientist named Don Merton came up with a clever plan to save the robin.

Don's plan was to use Chatham Island tits as foster parents to black robin chicks. He took eggs out of black robin nests and put them in incubators to keep them warm. Then he went by boat to another island where the tits lived, and put the robin eggs into tit nests. Meanwhile, back on Mangere Island the black robins laid more eggs.

After the eggs in the tits' nests hatched, the robin chicks were fed by the tit foster parents. When they were two weeks old Don took them back to their real robin parents, so they would realize they were robins and not tits.

Don's miracle was helped by a very special female robin, Old Blue. She got her name from the blue identification band on her leg. She lived to be at least 13 years old, which is more than twice as old as any other black robin, and she had many chicks. There are now over 130 black robins, and they are all descended from Don's friend Old Blue.

KAKAPO

When it comes to courting a female the male kakapo knows just how to put on a show. The kakapo is nocturnal, so it's a night-time performance.

First of all he hollows out some 'bowls' or arenas in the dirt. He connects these by a series of tracks, which he keeps smooth and tidy. When night falls he begins his performance. He puffs himself up until he looks like a huge balloon, and begins to call. His song is a deep, throbbing boom that echoes around the valleys.

A female kakapo hearing his boom may walk many kilometres to watch him dance. He stretches out his wings, and waves them like a butterfly. He sways back and forth and clacks his beak like castanets. If she is impressed by his dance the female may mate with him. It is now up to her to raise a family on her own.

The female builds a nest in a hole under a tree or a rock, where she lays two to four eggs. Once the fluffy white helpless chicks have hatched, she has to leave them on their own each night while she walks many kilometres to find food for them. At first she feeds them soft, juicy shoots. Later she feeds them rimu or kahikatea seeds, which are rich in protein.

The first kakapo chick seen this century was Snark, born on Stewart Island in 1981. Up until now, he has been living on Little Barrier Island but he will soon be transferred to Codfish Island.

The kakapo's name means night parrot. It is the world's heaviest parrot, weighing as much as a newborn human baby. The spray of whiskers on its owl-like face helps the kakapo find its way about at night. Cats and stoats can catch kakapo easily because the birds spend most of their time on the ground, have a strong sweet scent, and 'freeze' when surprised.

Kakapo used to live almost everywhere in New Zealand, but now there are only about 57 birds left. Scientists have moved them all to safe islands, and feed them extra food so they might be able to breed every year.

ROYAL ALBATROSS

Toroa

The mighty royal albatross is a true bird of the sea. It spends more than three-quarters of its life at sea, circling around and feeding in the southern oceans.

Every second year royal albatrosses return to dry land to raise just one chick with a life-long mate. When they first come back they can hardly walk, as their feet are soft and tender and aren't used to walking.

When they come ashore they greet their loyal mate with a 'sky call'. They point their bill to the sky, stretch out their wings and call with a harsh donkey-like noise.

It takes 11 months to raise a chick, and when the chick finally flies off from the nest it will be another four years before it touches land again.

Royal albatrosses have narrow wings that stretch 3 metres from wing tip to wing tip. These wings are perfect for gliding, and albatrosses soar for hours close to the sea surface, catching updraughts from the waves. In strong wind they can reach speeds of up to 140 kilometres an hour. They often rest on the sea surface, and to get airborne again will run up a wave and launch themselves off the top.

They use their strong, hooked beaks for grasping slippery squid and octopus as they come to the surface.

Royal albatrosses usually breed on remote islands, but one colony breeds on mainland New Zealand, only 50 kilometres from the city of Dunedin. Grandma, one of the birds that used to live in this colony, was about 63 years old when she disappeared – she was the world's oldest known wild bird.

Sailors used to believe that when old sea captains died they turned into albatrosses and wandered the cold seas forever. So they thought that killing an albatross would bring bad luck.

KIWI

The kiwi is a very special bird. It is related to the now extinct moa, and is more like an animal than a bird. It has an important part in our culture – we see it on stamps, coins and New Zealand-made goods, and we even call ourselves kiwis!

The flightless kiwi has wings the size of our little finger, and it has lost its tail. It is too heavy to fly, and its feathers are no use for flying – they are stiff, like dog hair, and they are tough, so they don't get damaged against the dirt walls of the kiwi's underground burrow.

Because the kiwi hides in burrows during the day, and comes out at night to feed, Maori called it Te Manu a Tane – the bird that Tane hid. Maori hunted kiwis using kuri, the now extinct Maori dog. The hunters fasted the day before the hunt, and the first kiwi caught was eaten by the hunters and their dogs.

As well as eating kiwi, Maori made valuable cloaks from the birds' hard-wearing feathers. Some of these old kahu kiwi are worn by Maori elders on special occasions.

Kiwi eggs are really big, about the size of six hen's eggs. Just before the female is ready to lay her one egg, her belly bulges so much it touches the ground. Once she has laid the egg in a special burrow, the male kiwi incubates it for two and a half months. When the chick is ready to hatch it kicks its way out of the egg using its powerful legs. When it is grown up it will use these strong legs and sharp claws to kick and fight.

Kiwis feed on earthworms, insects and berries. They have such good hearing they can hear the worms in the soil. They also use the nostrils on the end of their beak to sniff them out – they can smell the worm even when their beak is buried in the dirt. The whiskers at the base of their beak are very sensitive, and help the kiwi to find things in the dark.

Dogs are a major threat to kiwis, and can kill a bird simply by picking it up. Kiwis have weak chests because they don't have big wing muscles and they crush very easily. In 1987 a wild German Shepherd killed about 500 kiwis in a Northland forest. These days scientists working to protect kiwis use muzzled dogs to sniff the birds out for study.

BLUE DUCK

Whio

Whio! Whio! The Maori name for the blue duck, whio, sounds just like the shrill whistle of the male blue duck.

Unlike most ducks, which eat plants as well as insects, blue ducks eat only insects. They live in fast-flowing rivers and as they effortlessly glide up and down the rough rapids they grovel in and around stones, scraping off the larvae that cling to the rocks. The black flap at the tip of their bill protects it from the wear and tear of constant rubbing against rocks.

Each pair of blue ducks patrols up and down a kilometre or so of river that is their territory. They can fly well, but will more likely dive if disturbed.

Baby blue ducks are born with extra large feet, and from the moment they hatch they can swim as well as their parents. They scoot across the top of the water, and jump up on logs and rocks to rest.

The blue duck is sometimes called the blushing duck. It is the only bird in the world that blushes. Its pale bill turns pink when it gets excited.

Blue ducks are no longer found in many of the rushing streams and rivers they used to live in. Hydro dams have blocked up many rivers, and forest has been cleared along others, causing them to silt up and slow down. Another threat is the introduced trout, which competes for the same food.

In the water the parents watch carefully over the ducklings. The female stays close, calling to keep them together. The male trails behind, looking out for danger, such as gulls and shags, which might eat the ducklings.

MOREPORK

Ruru

The morepork is a great forest hunter. Like many owls, it hunts silently at night when most other birds are asleep.

Moreporks can fly without making a noise because their wing feathers have very soft edges. Only sometimes does their haunting cry give them away. Maori called them ruru, after the call they make, and thought the cry of a ruru was a bad omen. Europeans thought their call sounded like 'morepork'.

Most birds can't see in the dark, but moreporks have excellent night vision. Their large owl eyes are on the front of their head, just like ours, so they can judge distance. They can also look in every direction by swivelling their head almost right around. The staring eyes on Maori carvings are thought to be morepork eyes.

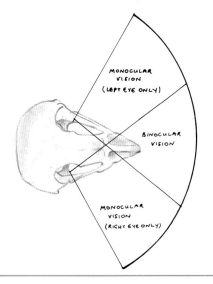

MONOCULAR VISION (LEFT EYE ONLY)

BINOCULAR VISION

MONOCULAR VISION (RIGHT EYE ONLY)

Moreporks also have fantastic hearing. One ear is slightly higher than the other, which helps them pinpoint where sounds are coming from. They use their sharp hearing to listen for insects and small animals such as lizards and sleeping birds, then they sneak up on their prey silently, and catch them by surprise.

Moreporks eat their food whole, but afterwards they cough up a pellet that contains all the bones, feathers and fur. They often leave these pellets on top of the fence-post or branch they have been sitting on. By pulling them apart with tweezers you can see what the morepork ate for dinner.

Moreporks nest in hollow trees or in the thick clusters of small plants growing in the crooks of branches. They lay two eggs in early summer. Once the chicks are three weeks old they perch at the nest entrance waiting for their parents to bring them food. When they are small, chicks are fed on insects or small pieces of bird. When they get bigger their parents drop whole birds for them to practise ripping up food with their claws and beaks.

KEA

The comical kea is a distinctive part of the South Island mountains. With its loud calls of 'keargh' this pigeon-toed clown soon makes itself known to skiers and trampers. Human belongings are a source of endless entertainment to this curious parrot, and it loves to poke, pry and stick its beak into everything.

For a lot of the time, however, keas are very private birds that go about their own affairs high in the mountains. In late winter, when there is still lots of snow around, the female kea builds a nest in a hollow tree or under a rock. She spends many weeks in the dark, quiet nest, incubating her eggs. Her mate hardly ever comes into the nest, but brings plant and insect food to the entrance for her.

Once the white fluffy chicks hatch, both parents have to work hard to feed them. Even after they leave the nest young keas continue to beg for food, and they can be very demanding. They spend a lot of time exploring their new surroundings, mimicking what their parents do and playing with each other. During this time the kea family moves around a lot, meeting other keas and discovering new places.

Once they are two or tree years old and on their own, keas spend a couple of years hanging around in kea gangs. These are the kea's 'teenage' years and

it is these 'gangs' that are most often seen around places such as skifields. While they come to grips with having to fend for themselves, 'teenage' keas often steal food from other keas.

By the time they are grown up, keas are experienced at finding food. They use their strong beak to dig up moss, drill into rotten wood for grubs, snip off leaves and delicately pick up berries. Their clawed feet also come in handy for picking up and holding objects. Leaves, berries and grubs, and even animal fat if it is available, all feature on the kea menu.

Even though life in the mountains is difficult and demanding, kea seem to thrive on it, and still have some time left for just fooling around.

SPOTTED SHAG

Parekareka

The spotted shag is the most striking and elegant of all the shags. In late winter spotted shags look particularly smart and dapper with their colourful breeding feathers.

They grow a head-dress of black crests, their dark brown eyes are ringed with blue 'eyeshadow', and the skin around their bill becomes a vivid green. Their coloured feet complete the outfit.

Once he is dressed for the part, a male spotted shag begins his courtship display. He raises his partly folded wings and flaps them. Then he points his closed bill at the sky, bends his head right back and lifts his tail.

Spotted shags rest and nest in colonies on steep sea cliffs, unlike river shags, which rest in tree tops. It takes a lot of skill to land on and take off from the narrow cliff ledges where they build their nests of seaweed, and it is surprising that the large chicks don't fall off these skinny ledges!

When the chicks are being fed they thrust their bill right up inside their parent's mouth to make sure they don't miss out on any of the regurgitated fish.

Spotted shags feed out at sea, in large groups of 500–2000 birds. They use their long hooked bill like a pair of tweezers to pick up small sardine-like fish.

KOKAKO

The kokako sings a most beautiful song. It sounds like a flute and an organ rolled into one, and early Europeans called it the 'organ bird'.

A Maori legend says the once silent kokako stole its beautiful voice from the bag moth, which is now silent. Another legend also paints the kokako as a thief. It was unhappy because it was plain grey, so it stole some dark feathers from its cousin the huia. But it only had time to steal enough for a black mask around its eyes before it was caught.

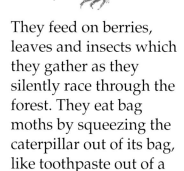

Kokako have bright blue pouches known as wattles next to their beak, and they belong to a group of birds known as wattle birds. The extinct huia, and the orange and black saddleback belong to the same ancient group of birds. Maori from the Ureweras say that the kokako got its blue wattles by rubbing against a bright blue mushroom found on the forest floor.

They feed on berries, leaves and insects which they gather as they silently race through the forest. They eat bag moths by squeezing the caterpillar out of its bag, like toothpaste out of a tube.

Kokako are poor fliers, but they make up for this by being great climbers. They leap and bound through the canopy and up tree trunks like squirrels, using the branches as a ladder. Once they are in the tree tops they glide back down again.

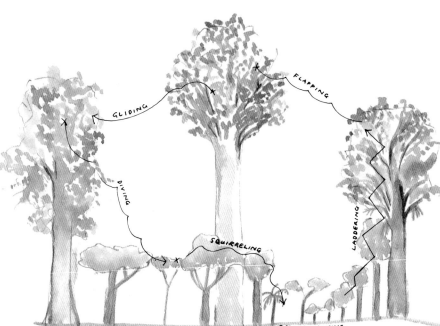

Cat could hear loud snoring. He crept
farther into the room. In the corner,
a giant dog was fast asleep. Cat filled
his bag with pet food and tiptoed away.
He climbed back down the beanstalk.

At the top of the beanstalk, Cat found himself in a strange land where everything was enormous.

He sneaked inside a huge castle to look around. He came across a room full of golden cans of pet food!

The next morning an enormous
beanstalk had grown in the
backyard. Cat grabbed his bag
and began to climb it.

The kokako's nest is built in the crook of a tree or in the top of a tree fern. When a parent feeds its chicks it pours out the berries, which tumble into the chicks' open beaks like coins pouring out of a slot machine.

Blue-wattled kokako are now found only in a few areas of tall forest in the North Island. Their South Island cousins with orange wattles are now probably extinct.

ACKNOWLEDGEMENTS

The author wishes to thank those scientists who helped with the information on specific birds, Alison Ballance for editing the text so beautifully, Geoff Arnold for his inspiring lessons on bird painting and Simon Høgh and Mark McGuire for assisting with the computer layout. Thanks also to Tom Beran and Maria Jungowska for overseeing the initial stages of this book.

REFERENCE BOOKS

Best, Elsdon. *Forest Lore of the Maori*. Dominion Museum/Polynesian Society, Wellington. 1942.

Butler, David and Merton, Don. *The Black Robin Story*. Oxford University Press, Auckland. 1992.

Harding, Mike. "Blue Duck — Symbol of Wild and Untamed Waters", *Forest and Bird* Vol. 22. No. 4, pp. 22–26.

Merton, Don. "The Chatham Island Robin", *Forest and Bird* Vol. 21. No. 3, pp. 14–19.

Moon, Geoff. *The Birds Around Us*. Heinemann, Auckland. 1979.

Moon, Geoff and Lockley, Ronald. *New Zealand's Birds*. Heinemann, Auckland. 1982.

Morris, Rod and Smith, Hal. *Wild South*. TVNZ/Century Hutchinson, Auckland. 1988.

Morris, Sandra and Moon, Geoff. *The Kingfisher*. Heinemann, Auckland. 1985.

Oliver, W. *New Zealand Birds*. AH and AW Reed, Wellington. 1958.

Peat, Neville. *The Incredible Kiwi*. TVNZ/Random Century, Auckland. 1990.

Peat, Neville and Gaskin, Chris. *The World of Albatrosses*. Hodder and Stoughton, Auckland. 1991.

Peat, Neville and Gaskin, Chris. *The World of Penguins*. Hodder and Stoughton, Auckland. 1991.

Reader's Digest Complete Book of New Zealand Birds. Reader's Digest, Sydney, in association with Reed Methuen, Auckland. 1985.

Veitch, Dick and Cemmick, David. *Black Robin Country*. Hodder and Stoughton, Auckland. 1985.

Published by Reed Children Books, an imprint of Reed Publishing(NZ) Ltd, 39 Rawene Road, Birkenhead, Auckland

Copyright ©1994 Sandra Morris
First published 1994
ISBN 1 86948 804 0
This edition published 1998

All right reserved. No part of this publication may be reproduced or transmitted in any form or by any means, electronic or mechanical including photocopy, recording, or any information storage and retrieval system, without permission in writing from the publisher.

Designed by Sandra Morris
Printed in Hong Kong